ROSES&RAVENS
SEARCH FOR SOMETHING

a book of poetry
CHRISTIAN MICHAEL

RAVENS AND ROSES: SEARCH FOR SOMETHING

Scroll Media Company
www.scrollmedia.org

This is a work of poetry.

ISBN-13: 978-0692503423 (Scroll Media)
ISBN-10: 0692503420

Printed in the United States of America

DEDICATION

To Life
For you have seen
All the dreams
By all the means

And all the hope
By all the strains
Till all lie down
And give their names

And to Edgar Allan Poe,
because Edgar Allan Poe.

COMING

Come to me, my son to me
Asking of thy love from thee
Wishing in my olden day
Of my children's greatest praise
And of what beyond me lay

Wonder in the future's light
Within my only daily right
And asking if
When my light will end

The dark is growing faster still
To test the strength of my will
To see if I have nothing left
What inside me have I kept
To help me cross the hill

CHRISTIAN MICHAEL

At the blankness of the wall
I will not give in and fall
And if I go to devil's due
I make an oath to take it all

How will I beget the night?
Of everything so good and sin
When splitting edges coming from light
And so will you in hell and heav'n

Strong it is a tale of me
Only sought of love from he
In which I had raised
Since sitting well upon my knee

Good bye my child
We must say adieu
Remember me always
My life was true

1996
Gray, Ga

I Have No Home

I have no home
This place of mine
It's not the spot
Still not the time

I have no home
This feeling's sure
It's deep within
And feels impure

I'm lost alone
No home for me
No refuge here
That covers me

It's not a roof
Nor walls around
That anchors heart
And soul to ground

I have no home
These walls are bare
No memories
Of lovely share

I have no bed
It's not for me
I lay in it
No peace believe

I have no home
For it is me
The blessed rest
Assurety

It has not come
This place I seek
The home I go
To finding me

CHRISTIAN MICHAEL

The darkness here
Is cold and sore
It's all around
Without my core

I have no home
For it, you see
Is not a place
Where you can be

I have no home
I seek her name
She's not a spot
Nor simple game

For home is heart
And I have none
She's a spectre
Ghosted run

Her lovely face
And son'rous arms
Have not yet found
My hollow heart

There is no home
For me just yet
It's not a place
It has no bed

For it's a she
And she's not here
I haven't found
Her in the clear

She's hiding just
Around the bend
This push in time
That has no end

I have no home
I have not seen
The lady love
To set me free

So I will wait
I have no choice
Time will not
Give me a voice

I have no home
But I believe
Yes she will come
One day, we'll see

June 9, 2015
San Antonio, Texas

THE FOCUS OF MY EYES

I will learn to live the moment
The only one in which I can live
There's no other space, in this old place
To find myself within

It's a little place called happiness
That eludes my every turn
Because I avail, in every tale
That newer thing to learn

So easy believe society
Is grander 'round the bend
But a waste of time, I spend my eyes
Search'ing another "when"

I'm here right now and here I'll be
I'll go no-where, in fact
Time will go as only it knows
My dreams in cataract

This moment is the surest thing
I'll find in all my wanders
It passes by just tics of time
And now no more it ponders

It cannot pass a second more
Than a moment will its waking
Nor here and now, nor word of how
The reasons for its taking

I took this trail of time and me
On roads around beyond
A mountain sure, for fate's own cure
For present's lonely fond

When will I gain and understand
The truth of living now
It now eludes in wistful moods
A thinker's endless how

To breathe this air and drink this wine
Get drunk this inner heading
Lose my way and find my day
And live in my own bedding

Like waves upon a rocky beach
Whit'ling quiet granite
A piece a day in its own way
Will move this massive planet

It's all I have, this place of mine
This momentary station
The second hand without a plan
But living its vocation

I can breathe in every time
And nothing more its moment
Embrace the now so soon without
This promontory roaming

I'll stop and stay in my own way
Appreciation hence
For all I am, this living man
And naught that I was then

For am I here and here is me
It's life itself, my prize
No more to change, but how it stays
The focus of my eyes

May 29, 2015
San Antonio, Texas

ADRIFT

I feel adrift out here in open sea
After conflicts, fight, unsureties
No longer sure what I'm to be
My hope is waning fast

These days have passed me by of late
I tried my best as not to wait
To find myself a plan and gate,
Away from peace I've cast

Normally I'd haul the anch
Drive down fears and drove this tank
Clear out a path for future's bank
But boldness didn't last

Instead I'm wheezy in the gut
Unsure if I would leave this rut
With nowhere else to go because
My strength is now aghast

I know that this will pass away
Like rainy seasons do some days
For floods will come and then shall wane
A memory soon past

I'm not out there just yet, or now
I'm still back here not reaching out
There is no strength to push the prow
My feet are holding fast

I wish the rain would soon return
To feel its cooler water burn
The air so chill and thunder churn
Like lower rumb'ling brass

It's okay to feel this way
It's part of growing every day
Because I've learned a lot of late
About how I am cast

So hard for surer gold I ran
After every, newer "could have been"
Ideas so good for other men
The journey was a blast

CHRISTIAN MICHAEL

But then had come epiphany
For what I'm better meant to be
Things fate had in store for me
Seem'ng less greener grass

And yet my lawn is still my heart
A tended hope not soon depart
It's just a risk to reach that start
I'd soon like much to pass

But can it be the things I dream?
Will hope revive the deeper mean?
Could I make it out to thee,
Where other writers hast?

This is what I'm 'signed to do
To weave a tale in something new
Carve a truth inside so, too
I wonder why I fast

Perhaps it seems too simple
This wrinkled fate in future's dimple
I'd have preferred so like an anvil
When heat is blowing blast

I can't deny the feelings, true
But I can say I'll try anew
Embracing who I am so due
And hope that it will last

I'm in it all the way this time
To weave my tales and sing my rhymes
And trust the one who made this mine
A ship's new sailing mast

In faith I'll walk to find my way
That northern star's sure light and sway
Upon this hope so now I'll pray
And hope it builds, at last

May 26, 2015
San Antonio

For Every Thought that Death Became

For every thought that death became
When the world was birthing men
And the blood that God reclaimed
Came the all-igniting sin

Death to all who came to pass
Who fought the peace we all had sought
Never ending things to task
On futures we had thought were bought

Life to those who kill our children
The only mercy they'll receive
Before the darkness burns without them
And a chance for their reprieve

Feasting on the whippered flesh
Of those who never came before
Yet promised us the needed rest
Then nailed us to the wooden floor

Cry us havok for the sins
Burn us dying for the pain
Roiling up from feet to chin
And screaming deep inside my brain

Kill the vesper in the marrow
Soon before the bone can break
When the pain forg-es us harrowed
And our life becomes too late

Burst the ground from neath our feet
Grandiose comes sunset gain
How the belfry cries defeat
And my soul is cursing lame

Deftly lose the ponder thinking
How to lose the demon's eyes
Where our fear can come to brinking
And drown us in personal lies

So lay me down to death tonight
One last jaunt before I cry
The greatest sleep we all alight
Before we wake again to die

September 4, 2006
Hampton, Va.

I Leave Complete

I caught the demon, he looks like me
He eats my soul from out my sea
He clings inside what thought was mine
He whispers here sweet sufferings

There he sits while I abide
And wait him out like morning Tide
And if I wish my life were mine
He reminds me like I lied

We look alike, this death and I
Like twins between a watchful eye
I might have wished to disalign
He twists my arm and makes me cry

I woke one morn to find him gone
I realize it far too long
I cried with joy but understood
His absence was a greater wrong

He left my soul but not alone
He took my spirit to the bone
He broke my faith with putrid lies
And now I sit, an empty home

The hole, you see, was not his work
The emptiness no simple flirt
He had come at my request
Widening had been his work

The rip, you see, was deeper still
Than demons could have hoped to fill
The gap sitting inside my chest
Was not my own by choice, or will

I had lost a love one day
I couldn't name the time or date
I only know it wasn't best
It didn't heal or soon relate

Instead I sought the open road
Not the simple travel hope
But opened a replacement quest
Duct-taped the hole and tied the rope

The demon came along one day
Sat inside and mat the hay
A horse in stable, bird in nest
He paved the way that I had made

Years went by that I could tell
I tried the ways that brav'ry yells
But soon enough began to fest
And sickness grew inside my well

I boiled o'er and soon became
A wilder horse now running lame
As if I needed more to show
How my passions grew my shame

Sitting here an empty bleed
A hollow house in greater need
My demon gone, and naught to show
The devil lost but no reprieve

It came to me I'd sought the wrong
The path I'd chosen wasn't long
It simply took a simpler hope
Humility to soon belong

CHRISTIAN MICHAEL

And all my pride had kept me there
Fearing that I'd have to share
Instead soon tying thicker rope
And stepping on the killer's snare

Fighting through the things that grew
From talking with someone who knew
How to pass the Slip'ry Slope
And walk away from death's own due

It took the time to learn myself
To see why I had chosen hell
To let the heart inside me show
How to get out from this well

Daddy wasn't there, you see
But Mommy loved especially
There are truths in mind, I know
But in the heart, it disbelieves

It cannot see the truth endured
That life right now is not before
There to here, how much I've grown!
But still inside a softer core

Here in this day I see the hope
I have a guide, he lowered rope
He'll show me how to walk the slope
To heal the crack inside my soul

It's time to leave my past behind
To kill the lion chasing time
Who in my dream was there to kill
So now's the chance to make it mine

I'm taking names and kicking ass
I'll cut your face and stab with glass
The demon leaves and I soon will
To vacate death before collapse

A perfect man I'll never be
Not part of higher design-ing
Life alive is like a mill
It grinds you up till you grow wings

The time has come to grow and fight
I'll make it through another night
I don't need an addiction's pill
I'll bare my soul, He'll wash it white

CHRISTIAN MICHAEL

And when I'm whole and fin'ly through
Have killed the demon, been renewed
My soul at peace and heart so still
I'll credit all my change to You

You're the hope I've always held
From life's own little heav's and hells
You are why I'm living still
It's secret I will always tell

So here's to life and living free
Of our own inner demon'ry
Addictions and the things we love
That kill inside the love we need

I will rise and make the toll
To slay the drag' and club the troll
Trusting in the One above
To seal the crack and become whole

It wasn't in me all alone
My flimsy skin or brittle bones
Together we might bear the shove
And soon will carry us on home

All the things I wish I could
Have healed before the way I should
I'll change before it's not enough
And past mistakes destroy what's good

It took awhile to get me here
Releasing all my inner fears
That sheathed my hand a razored glove
Broke the dam and poured my tears

I stand before you here tonight
A different man in different light
From sinly smooth to purely rough
It's better now to feel so right

My soul is healed, the wound is closed
It even pours a healing prose
But everything I've spoken of
Has come to pass through broken roads

There was no easy way beyond
The choices I was left to pond'
I saw that I was not so tough
I made the choice to right the wrong

CHRISTIAN MICHAEL

I take a knee, my time is done
My words will end, my battle won
The time was due to change my stuff
Time to change into a son

A man before fell in defeat
Stands now healed on two wide feet
My soul secure whom I've become
I came here broke, I leave complete

June 8, 2011
Warner Robins, Ga.

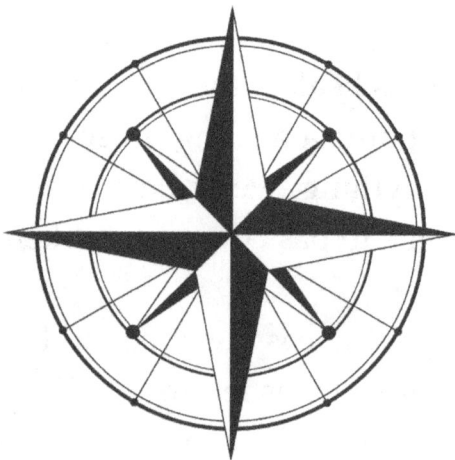

I Still Believe

I am the dreamer, I still believe
That hope in love will bring reprieve
That hope in God will grow belief
That truth in Him might lay relief

The path beyond could lay the wake
This sordid, single soul to take
With lights alive soon as I wake
The hope of nothingness soon break

And cooling couling jets to prove
There's nothing more like I could do
To offer hope in all I've done
And find my peace like finding you

It's still my fault, this death aligning
In the bosom's core refining
And in the gap we'll taste the run
With others over us divining

June 1, 2013
Denver, Colo.

There is Hope

There is hope
There is dreaming
There are things I'm still receiving
While the dead have all the seeming
This poem here is late

For the words of this old rhyme
I declare, it is the time
And still while I'm reminded
That this story's lovely gate

Might still come between us
But if you will now believe this
I'll declare that something grievous
Might still happen anyway

Let us talk
Let us rant
Of the things we don't lament
And tales we yet recant
Of the evening's early sway

Don't forget,
Lest we sweat
Of the world life still begets
With you and your regrets
I'll declare it dead today

Speak me whispers
Speak the tispers
And the other words unsaid
While you lie upon your bed
And the sweat has yet dried off

But the sickness
Oh is quickest
While the rest of us are sleeping
And the shadows still are creeping
But really, just a cough

CHRISTIAN MICHAEL

Now with wonders
Or those blunders
The words I've yet remembered
Or the fires left untendered
In the heart I once held sway

Touch your lips
With this old kiss
You don't have to be remiss
Round the friends you've not dismissed
And the liberty in space

Could the times
The ones are mine
And the cloudy sauntered savvy
With their lovely amble gladly
Keeping softer stately pace

Hear the words
Speak the nerds
I spoke when no one listened
Though the gold within me glistened
And no one seems to miss 'em
I would dare to comprehend

That the lace
Is not this way
Rhyming center staffer
With all the raucous laughter
And the dogs are running faster
Just a turn around the bend

Will you speak
Still reprieve
Till I barely could retrieve
Any living human being
In this wretched, cursed fiend
I would have you on my lap

CHRISTIAN MICHAEL

But a kiss
So more than this
Of the subtle, classy nature
Of a woman smart and greater
Than the brunettes and the bakers
It's really just a map

And in the end
It's not a friend
Who captures every moment
With the loudest standing groaning
Or the dying mirthful moaning
Inside the love you make

Leave the sex
It's this perplexed
With words so intertwining
Like love in sheetly vining
For nature's own divining
It's this that makes it great.

October 30, 2010
Hampton, Va.

For Life Alive
is Autumn Brown

Here the fight begins again
With morals intertwining sin
And all I cry when dead within
Is asking if we ever win

What's the point of fighting on
With greater consequences gone
And all bescreaming it gone wrong
Speaks of death in wishful song

To fight the war and say goodbye
Like victory on-ly to die
For days on end we're left to cry
To start again within his eyes

What is all the struggle for?
Seek we favor at your door?
Who are we to ask for more,
The undeserv-ed on the floor?

CHRISTIAN MICHAEL

All the good and bad intwined
Lifting life and breaking time
Death to sin and life to crime
Kill the calf before we lie

Speak to me you neutral 'tween
Tell me what defiance brings
Is there truth in heaven's being
We the much, our minds unclean

Smoke the hills and burn the caves
From out the mouth, the crest of babes
And then we die to find our place
As our strength arrives in waves

Why are we alone to choose?
Then punished if it isn't you?
To blackmail rights and trim the news
Makes as bad as you know who

Benevolence I thank you for
And peace alive, I ask for more
But I deserve to be uncored
According to the word you poured

If so evil we might seem
And with us you wish to be
How can we correct the seed
That gave us all that carnal need?

Cry thee havok, for all around
Come the demons to the ground
In every place come grateful sound
For life alive is autumn brown

The coldest summer threatens me
Here confusion reigns supreme
To end the fight and become free
Sleeping loud comes better spree

Forgive me all the things I do
I really tried to stop for you
But bound to it, I say, in truth
Has left me feeling unt'wards you

How can I reclaim my place
Or should I try at all, today?
Should I come to find your way
Or will you meet me in my craze?

Let the fires burn me through
I will fight to come to you
But is it worth the death so due
And what's the cause if word is true?

Cloudy comes the day before
From Paris kings to Russian whores
Who alike knows what's in store
For death alone can end for sure

So here we break the tides of time,
Beating on in rhythm's rhyme
Wond'ring who will call me mine
In hopes that peacefully I'll find

As God becomes the point unsure
Begging one another's cure
Save me from this moral sewer
And cleanse me from myself impure

June 22, 2007
Marietta, Ga.

Grace and Favor With You All

May the God of heaven's light
Stand beside you big and tall
As you travel through the night
Grace and favor with you all

I pray the peace of heaven-sent
With courage in you for the call
We are straightly now in-bent
Grace and favor with you all

For-get not the laws of God
Remember that you'll always fall
For He will go where e'er you trod
Grace and favor with you all

His mercy is as new as babes
Born and wrapped in mother's shawls
Never early nor so late
Grace and favor with you all

CHRISTIAN MICHAEL

Pray a simple prayer tonight
In your room or in the hall
God will make your wrongs to right
Grace and favor with you all

Here we're left in broken souls
With no way our own future stall
With only One to fill these holes
Grace and favor with you all

As far as you may journey now
China, Burma, or Nepal
I need not know the why or how
Grace and favor with you all

So as I leave your bed tonight
With dreams of God to leave in awe
He will bring you by His side
Grace and favor with you all

April 19, 2005
Hampton, Va.

I Will Dance
with Death

I will dance with Death
For Death has danced with me
I will dance with Death
For it has set me free
I will dance with Death
So all of you may know
As far as you dance with Death
No farther shall you go.

November 23, 2003
Biloxi, Ms.

May Your Heart
Come Out of Night

Darkness does thee now enfold
For future night entombed in mind
Whispers softly of the moon
Where better times were out of line

Were the white and black to meet
Depth of hate and littered strength
Worshiping the saints of yore
And the demon's speech at length

Where the grayscale scrapes the stark
Where the times are left alone
Tears alone are former smiles
Now to die in fitful groan

Let the quiet seep inside
Embrace the stillness of the night
As the stars we stare upon
Give to us the quipple light

Rest in peace, dear quiet girl
Fret upon these things no more
Loneliness will breed despair
And make your rest upon the floor

Smile now for all delight
Let the speaker tell his sight
For as your darkness comes to rest
May your heart come out of night

October 2, 2006
Hampton, Va.

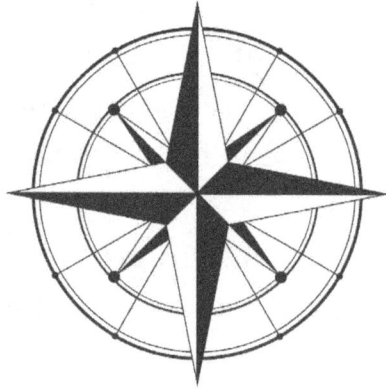

Sleep Well, My Darling, Sleep Well

Sleep well, my darling, sleep well
For we run from heaven and fall into hell
Living off of what we yet can tell
Our senses are off or it really smells

Are we ready to stave off the night
The things in which we always delight
But truer said from fear in flight
Nobody sleeps till we see the light

Could we agree on the things we decide
Now that I've told you I beg you to side
Understand all of those things I don't hide
And leave all the rest of it lying besides

Tell me the stories of all of the old
But only the tales from which I can make gold
It doesn't matter to the bodies left cold
They turn to dust while their money I fold

Tell me of things that you wish I would do
Then beg me to do them because it's for you
Let us begin with our beginnings new
And then you will tell me of you that is who?

CHRISTIAN MICHAEL

Then you would threaten with all of your power
Newly acquired from early this hour
Over me now your desire to tower
Leaves me no choice but to work and to shower

Have you forgotten the begotten rules?
News of how better we use our own tools
And you're left there standing 'mongst cities of
fools
My word, and to think, that I thought you were
cool!

Doesn't my lord walk away from it all?
Needing of nothing but us at his call
No need to run or his enemies stall
For when he sits down he remains just as tall?

August 12, 2007
Marietta, Ga.

TAKE ME IN YOUR ARMS TONIGHT

Take me in your arms tonight
Let me sleep by candlelight
For all the pain that I've endured
Just say it'll be alright

My heart feels like it has been
Torn in twain and then again
Let me know your touch is pure
And I'm forgiven of my sin

It doesn't feel like I should be
Thrown away and trampled free
I thought that I had done my best
But you once said that is was me

February 15, 2004
Newport News, Va.

The Nakedness of Soul

I have found a moment's stare
Caught alone and unawares
Where to find where I would go,
When all within too soon laid bare

The nakedness of soul now found
When all inside is now laid down
I can't escape what I now know
And my faults played in the Round

Could the world have turned on me?
Enslave by who I used to be?
Pull me down and take me low?
So I could never feel as free?

When does all the fighting end?
Against the world and then within?
When did I become the foe?
Ball and chained up to my sin?

For worlds alone are in my eyes
And it is all I have to cry
We will reap from what we sew
Here then on until we die

August 17, 2006
Hampton, Va.

For Every Time
We Thought To Say

For every time we thought to say
Things we never stopped to think
Maybe now correct mistake
Or bring a friendship to it's brink

Come again and say aloud
Better things to think about
Say it fast and say it now
Speak it soft or with a shout

But say your peace to me this day
In any manner you can find
Say it in the bestest way
Never more to hide behind

Peace between a brothers two
Or for a sister's three
This is better all for you
And better, yes, for me

So all around the table say
Sorry to the one you've hurt
Make things right in your own way
And make it down and sure

So my friends in peace I leave
You all to find your hope
Better there than in a swing
From a friendly hang-man's rope

April 19, 2005
Hampton, Va.

THIS TILL YOU OPEN YOUR EYES

Can we all agree to disagree
On things that we can never see?
In places we'd ever want to be
And then to talk of things achieved?

Let's remember places lost
And together count the cost
In English accents say the past
Is now exactly just as fast

So for things we've yet to feel
And the pains we've yet to heel
Before the Gods we're not to kneel
Our souls are lost and still to steel

Daily words of lovers' arms
Lost forever nature's harm
Count once more and sound alarm
I'll not fall into your charms

The depth within is keeping close
Things I don't want you to know
And though you have already chose
You can always count me as foe

Steps once more on dusty paths
And you don't know where I am at
For I have hid the hide of that
In front of you where you had spat

Leave me yet to find the truth
And I will leave it here with you
To find yourself where you were too
Far too gone to say the sooth

I know that light is brighter still
But only if you have the will
To stand aloft and sitting still
To face the demon as it kills

So alone I leave you here
Left alone with all your tears
Until your strength can face your fears
I will leave you to your years

So open eyes before you fall
You have fallen open tall
And while you're not quite here at all
I will leave the winter call

Goodnight, goodnight and goodbye
I have seen the broken cry
While you refuse to see the why
This til you open your eyes

April 19, 2005
Hampton, Va.

WILL YOU BE MY VALENTINE

Never let the memory
Of the Father fade from thee
For the days you've yet to see
Let not your judge be history

For the days we lost ourselves
To fight who fought and rang our bell
For those who kissed and wouldn't tell
Now to come and break the spell

Never lose sweet innocence
For you should never need repense
Chase the wrong over the fence
And live a life of sweeter sense

Against the pains of yesterday
And the unknown future ways
I know that you will always say
The better thing to do is pray

So as the days are passing time
I'm not asking you be mine
But in the very friendly kind
Will you be my Valentine?

February 2005
Hampton, Va.
For my friend, Victoria

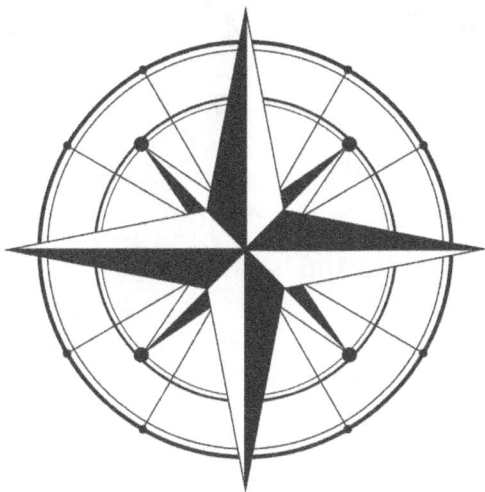

Inauguration

To the morning, to the night
Here we sleep by candlelight
To evening, to the dawn
Think of living now as one
To the waking, to the sleep
Now to live in safer keep
Now to quiet, now to speak
For the ever living sweep

February 19, 2005
Hampton, Va.

Touch of Serenity

In a moment's touch serenity
I find myself awake
I still do not find answers here
I fear it is too late

What's there to appease my soul?
And comfort weary heart?
Caught between the fighting kings
My eyes see only dark

I've no control of things around
I reach out in the ink
Alone nowhere on this small bed
Left only to think

Thoughts and thoughts, they murder me
Stirring foul emotion
Love and touch and closeness fare
As in this lonely ocean

2002
Monterey, Ca.

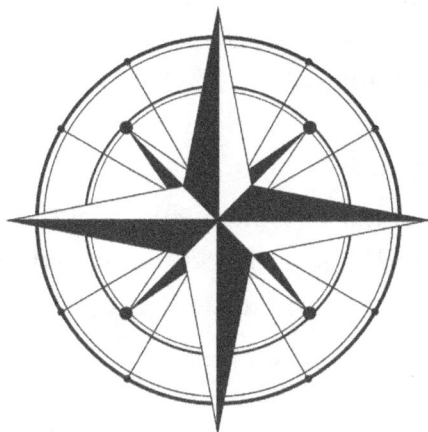

And Us
Will Find Peace

Into the darkness of depth and of change,
with faith by my side while enemies rage,
to find hope in the night and God in the heart,
to end all atrocities before they impart.

We'll still seek the heroes and cut them all down,
They called themselves heroes burning love to the
ground,
and I say that freedom is life's truest form,
security to wind and your fear to a storm

Amen to all prayers and be gone to all demons,
for life's ups and downs have their own living seasons,
nor will I seek those who sate the here now,
while the roots still inside are what keep me around.

I might need a doctor and I might need a friend,
I refuse to let either become my own end.
And when I find time and God comes to find me,
only we can find us, and us will find peace.

August 28, 2009
Marietta, Ga

I am the Dreamer

I am the dreamer, for what shall I dream?
Of what mysteries, or sadducees, or killers in seam?
The mind's own eye is paralyzed by what I've never known,
Just let me wish, for yours, oh dish, and now we're halfway home!

For you I'd say, most anything, to keep you here with me
But more's to come, said weary drum, oh sister, don't believe?
It's not the words or happy coils, that leave you lying there
But all mistakes we failed to brake, when time was drawing 'ere

And nights beyond, the simpleton, I knew it was too soon
For rabbits die, inside the eyes, with top hats, then, and brooms
Alice wandered down the hole, with nothing left to see
But all who'd passed before her, the regretted symphony

I've dreamt of days when future plays were failing at their form
The lights were out, and all about, the weather took her warmth
Then there you were, oh moment's pine, the thing desired most
What will you do, when yours own true, is really holy's ghost?

The clouds around, and all through town, Aurora's own behest
A dream of dreams, of finer things, the colors from the west
Her hair was fine, her shoulders true, her eyes were like the night
When winter's dance upon the sky had kept the world abright

CHRISTIAN MICHAEL

And here I sit, with things to do, of hopes I can't yet breathe
All I want, from stop to saunt, is you right here with me
I'll dream of you, till world turns blue, you're now no make-believe
But until then, I'll say amen, and pray for just reprieve

The sky's aloud with singing now, a voice not heard for years
Of one I knew, a sailor true, upon the crashing fears
It took no time and held no rhyme but'a lengthy poem t'was
For all my work, my stupid perk, and growing facial fuzz

April 11, 2011
Warner Robins, Ga.

For All the Words

For all the words you've now bequeathed
The meaning here now lies between
The truth you buried in the read
The life, the death and soul of me

I think of me instead of you
I worship self above the truth
It's time to change the life I knew
A chance to be somebody new

Here's a task I cannot face
I'm not alone, but I am fake
The farce I've been here takes the cake
Oh God, please help me change my ways

Lent for all is lent for none
Change your action, lose the son
Does it help the soul of one
To follow crowds on cliffside runs?

CHRISTIAN MICHAEL

Change your heart to change your soul
Change your thinking on the whole
Breathe new words and break your mold
It's time to steal what death had stole

How much longer will you wait?
To pass beyond the unlocked gate
Been sitting there since you were late
Unlocked, untied, unleashed to date

April 24, 2011
Warner Robins, Ga.

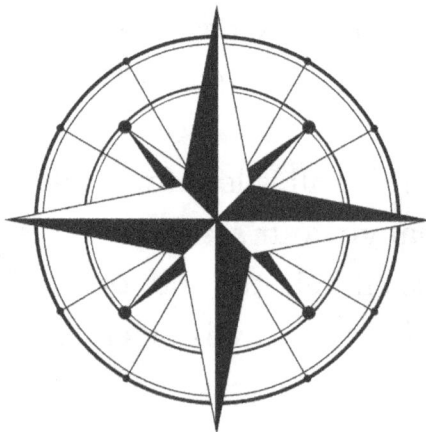

I Am Dreamt

I am dreamt of your years
The passing of days
The longing of tears
And the hereaft dismayed

Bereft of the moment
When here I between
The catching of angels
And sweet memories

For hoping of wonders
I've never yet laid
The castles of men
Or the moon on display

Dreaming of fireflies
So soon at the moon
Where hopes are in-soared
Inside my cocoon

CHRISTIAN MICHAEL

What beauties left standing
What hopes in my heart
Of seeing your eyes
In worlds far apart

I've seen you in sleeping
The flashes I see
A soul full of fire
And'a mind men made keen

Hope beyond hope
For your reasons of reason
Illogical tides
Ill-be-gotten seasons

What dreams you have made
What things we had hoped
To die and to feel
To me soon elope

When will I find you
Oh highest of hires
The work set before me
A passion inspired

But you are no workplace
No toil, or snare
No feelings of virtue
No bury to spare

Inside are the wildest
The beasts in the seam
Sudden disposes
I think it might mean

The smoke still here passes
The fog in the morn
The sound of the water
And thrill of the born

Feelings of wanting
For more than the flesh
More than imagine
Or writing, or tests

CHRISTIAN MICHAEL

There's something about you
I cannot yet tell
For I have not seen it
But felt it so well

It's in-side you waiting
For someone like me
To light up your candle
To burn in fu-ry

These words may not mean much
For ever I dream
Of the time of your eyes
The smile, it's mean'g

Years passing slowly
A wonder is this
My age is a story
From time's gentle kiss

And here is the hope
The wonder and feel
When all that about us
Ceases its real

Know that in heaven
A spirit besides
Will walk in the angels
Her smile so wide

Tis not of the cherubs
Or spirits from then
The time of the sera-
Phim lost unto men

Here is the dreamer
I sleep here at last
A moment to whisper
A long sorrow's cast

I'm hoping in waiting
And hoping to heal
That I would be whole
By the time you are real

CHRISTIAN MICHAEL

Here to the sunrise
The coming of you
The light of my life
When you sprinkle the dew

And whispering waiting
Is never befixed
Onto the graveyards
Of previous sticks

Dream of the happy
And 'mare of the sad
'Spose of the unknown
Detest all the bad

I'll be here waiting
There's a sheet made of glass
Separate separate
'Midst coat racks and hats

I'll be here watching
Till the time becomes right
When the angels are paving
All stillness of night

Here comes the moment
And there goes the past
I'm stepping to-wards you
I'll be there at last

Let nothing between us
Let nothing, I say
I will be with you
And nothing delay

The hope of my hope
And faith yet made cast
I will be with you
You'll be here.
    At last.

May 14, 2011
Warner Robins, GA

Not One
for Forsaking

For all you wish to take that dream
In the pathway of your making
The timing of the holy one
Is not one for forsaking

If you wish to rush ahead
And leave the mind behind
You had best be now prepared
To see your faith decline

Trusting God is not for lust
For things you never had
But resting in his timing thus
To let him make your bed

The faith of children in his hand
Comes not from our own making
Not of life or efforting
Or forcefully for taking

For all the good we see in life
We wish would never end
The presence of the Holy One
Is more than ending sin

Momentarily we wait
In every single instant
Learning all about his gait
To imitate persistence

Pause your rush and leave it be
Trust in His eternity
Days so short in life so long
There's nothing so importantly

As letting him direct your path
The road of his own making
The one in whom you trust to lead
The one not worth forsaking

December 3, 2011
Vacaville, CA

CHRISTIAN MICHAEL

Twas the Night ... at an Undisclosed Location

Twas the night before Christmas, at an undisclosed location
Not a creature was stirring through services station

All the Airmen were moving, out to cadillacs
To empty their bladders and Skype on their macs

The Indy was empty of all but the mids
The SF's on shift who'd yet been to bed

And I was still sleeping with no cots to spare
In a room with an A/C as loud as a snare

When out of the window I sure was to hear
Refuelers returning from FOBs far and near

I sprang from my bed afraid I was late
Where was my uniform, my belt and my cape

I ran from my room and long down the hall
Screaming my lungs to the death of us all

The sun had arisen at 535
And looked like late evening at so bright a light

The BPC sat there with Elysium's lure
But only the officers could feel so assured

...

December 24, 2012
Al Udeid Air Base, Qatar

(Writer's Note: This is as far as I could think of at the time, and by the time of this publishing, I've forgotten what else to add to it! Life is funny.)

CHRISTIAN MICHAEL

Here I Beg Thee, Now

Here I beg thee, now
Stand there now to pray
That we together now will make
Our passage through this day

And when the night is over
And the stars are all aligned
Find me in the wading wind
Our souls will entertwine

That we might find forever
Waiting in the winds
Escaping from the rising sun
And holy fear within

And when the day has passed us
The evening soon to come
The thunder of the angel eyes
Beating weary drums

So soon now for the taking
Our world so long, so passed
Had once called us by other names
Before we thought to last

Forever now will never go
Where we once thought it might
But in the hopes and aching throws
Will shine upon the light

CHRISTIAN MICHAEL

But we will fin'ly make it
Like lovers stars have made
To see the light beyond the peak
The sun inside its cave

Here now wait forever
A chance it might come pass
It's not about eternity
But how our love will last

Weep not now for passing
For death will never be
An end to hearts so hoped inside
For life, like it will need

Denver, Co.
December 27, 2014

INSIDE OF A MOMENT

Inside of a moment
Lies eternity
And now where we are waiting
Our souls are flying free

On another playing field
Competition is our game
But something else is on my list
A thing not near so tame

A firefight, a blitzkreig
Battle 'suing here
Nothing left inside but will
And strength hold'ing our fears

Misunderstanding what I have
Can kill me in the end
Take away my only life
To leave regrets within

A turning moment here again
A step, direction's move
A dying chance to save myself
Pulled from morbid groove

Next in line and last to know
I'm smiles and chagrins
Whoever would have ever thunk
I'd be the first one in

2002
Monterey, Ca.

Death to Final Words Beyond

Death to final words beyond
Caught again and it's all wrong
Lifting up my hands to pray
Dreaming of the moon long gone

Feel the wind upon your face
Like water spinning in a vase
Swirling like a game in play
Ball to child in endless chase

Swirling leaves in dance tonight
Forest breeze in firelight
The owl's eyes in branch'es sway
Day until the morning sight

CHRISTIAN MICHAEL

Grace me so I fell you near
I'm afraid in heavy tears
Lead me on to chosen day
Strength in weakness growing here

Left alone to tell the truth
Though undeserved and quite uncooth
Working hard to drive away
Fears kept up inside this booth

Grant me knowledge in my home
Better young and then be grown
Serve it burnt on silver tray
Just so as I'm not alone

Father, in your aging glory
Set me down and tell a story
Tell me of the better way
Bittersweet and cleanly gory

Living life with gentler gender
Starting fires in love-soaked tender
Being able just to say
My wife and I were warm in winter

Confident in who I am
In dry Brazil or wet Siam
Wherever my head might lay
I know and do all that I can

Slow me down and teach me fast
Grind it down so it will last
So I can keep my fear at Bay
and myself within me cast

I'm not afraid but I could cry
Tears from skin are running dry
Life sometimes seems all too gray
Simplicity is knowing why
Simplicity is knowing why

2002
Monterey, Ca.

CHRISTIAN MICHAEL

Man of Sea

O' to be a great man of sea
To ride in a ship and always to be
A sailor, a warrior, a great Navy man
To ride and conquer almost every land
And be strong in the face of our enemy

Winds they come and arrive in a gale
The ship streaks on as sleek as a whale
A sea before me, the land behind
I have many supplies and plenty of time
The breath of the ocean a sailor's first tale

Ship of a querious flag appears
A solitary tower adorned in her fear
My crew became ready for anything new
A command of the slightest to ready their due
'Gainst any unseemly com-ing privateer

Alone to the ocean in motion we went
'Gainst squalls who might stall so tall in their bent
Who crash, who bash, who fall on our hulls
And knock aside sailors absent secure pulls
Slide away, slide away, the oceanside sent

Here, we'll bow alone to the sea
The lady herself as so rolling she'll be
A witness to sit this fine journey she'll watch
As we fight for the waves and the pirates a lot
Before she deigns resting in something serene

Love, it's not something I know
Beyond the fine woman who hastens our go
The ocean of lovely so far and so near
She'll baptize a baby while sprink'ling our fear
Whilst keeping our wistfulness tightly in tow

See, how the foreigner comes
Not a single sound made, nor beating of drum
An ambush awaits as she pulls alongside
Exploding with pirates and merciless cries
We're ready and steady as if we were one

CHRISTIAN MICHAEL

'Arms' is the cry to the sky I have made
My crew now beset by dangerous blades
But there is a vet'ran in e-ver-y man
They stand alongside their brothers and friends
While spirits of anguish arise from the wade

'Go,' they now cry to themselves
Far from the stories of blood my men tell
For each of them wouldn't let any of fear
Tell them their futures of vagabonds near
And laughed with the angels as brigands so fell

So, to be a captain of men
I lead the ship sailing through storms and the
wind
There is something about how the ocean she
shines
While all of us watch with our hearts so aligned
To forget a memory whisper behind

O' to be a great Man of Sea

1994, Macon, Ga.
2015, San Antonio, Texas

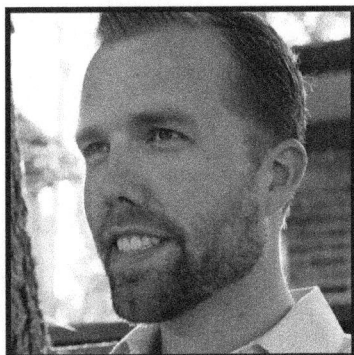

About the Author

Christian Michael has moved 46 times (so far), lived in eleven states and two countries. A military veteran, voice actor, graphic and web designer, blogger, poet, musician and entrepreneur in-progress, Christian focuses on the journey in life, translating those lessons and adventures into his fiction.

For more information on Christian, visit his web site and connect with him on social media.

Look for Christian's newest book, "Stardusk," a sci-fi novella coming out later in 2015.

www.ChristianMichael.org
www.ScrollMedia.com
www.ScrollBookstore.com
www.facebook.com/cmichaelwriter

More by the Author

Last Battle: Dusk of Xanthar (2010)

The Moving Book:
Manage Your Migration (2014)

Stardusk (2015)

www.ingramcontent.com/pod-product-compliance
Lightning Source LLC
Chambersburg PA
CBHW020556030426
42337CB00013B/1116